Hitler

The rise and fall of one of history's most destructive men

Table of Contents

Introduction

Thank you for taking the time to pick up this book all about Hitler.

This book covers Adolf Hitler and the destructive life that he lived. In the following chapters, you will learn about Adolf Hitler's early years, and how he came to form the extreme beliefs that he is remembered for.

Also documented is exactly how he rose to power in Germany, and the level of destruction that he was responsible for during the 2nd world war.

At the completion of this book you will have a good understanding of Hitler's life, how he came to be, the amount of impact he had on the world, and ultimately how he was defeated.

Once again, thanks for choosing this book, I hope you find it to be an informative read!

Chapter 1: Early Life

"Those who want to live, let them fight – and those who do not want to fight in this world of eternal struggle do not deserve to live."
—Adolf Hitler

Adolf Hitler was born on April 20, 1889 in Braunau am Inn (on the Austrian border), nestled about 65 miles from Munich and 30 miles to the north of Salzburg. His father Alois Hitler was a middle-level officer in the customs department. Born as Alois Schickelgruber, his father assumed the name to Hitler in 1876, the Christian name of his step-father who married his mother a few years after his birth (Alois was born out of wedlock).

Questionable Family Lineage

Alois Hitler's illegitimacy has been hugely speculated throughout history, with suggestions that Hitler's lineage was Jewish. However, there has never been credible evidence to support Hitler's controversial descent. His grandfather was believed to be either the man who was wedded to his grandmother or the man's brother. This makes tracing his biological family roots a huge task.

Alois, an Austrian customs officer, was able to offer his kin a reasonably comfortable life. However, his relationship with Adolf wasn't known to be very cordial owing to Alois' foul temper and arrogance. Hitler's step-father was believed to highly conceited, brash and obnoxious. Alois often vented out all his ire on the children, which didn't go down too well with Adolf during his formative years.

Early Education

Once he completed primary education, his father enrolled him to Realschule, which emphasized science and technological subjects as opposed to a conventional curriculum. Hitler hated his time there and made no bones about the fact in every account of his early life. Though he was exceptional in primary school, his grades dropped drastically in the new institute. His grades never picked up again.

At 16, he dropped out of school. Though he had the option to pursue higher education, Hitler opted out of any further academic education. Much of his personality has been attributed to the losses Adolf Hitler faced early in his life. Many of his siblings didn't survive beyond their childhood. He lost his father at 14. Later, Hitler's mother would face an early death from breast cancer, which was one of the biggest losses he faced at a young age.

After he dropped out, his family moved to Linz, the then-capital of Upper Austria, in 1898. Adolf Hitler rebelled against his father to pursue a visual arts vocation, though they later wanted him to be a part of the Habsburg civil service. After his father's demise, Hitler ended up convincing his mother Klara Hitler to let him become an artist. When his mother was bed-ridden and dying of breast cancer in 1907, Hitler took the Vienna Academy of the Arts entrance exam. He failed to get accepted in the institute. After Klara's death in 1907, he packed his bags for Vienna in the hope of giving the Academy of Arts acceptance another shot.

Vienna Diaries

Hitler resided in Vienna from February 1908 to May 1913. He grew up in a middle-class background with little contact with Jews in the Habsburg state. Habsburg housed several German nationalists who had expressed strong disappointment over the fact that the 1871-founded German Empire excluded the predominantly German-speaking Habsburg Monarchy.

There are not many references to his early years in Vienna available. However, according to various historic accounts, he sought residence in several shelter homes throughout the region and led a rather impoverished life. He squandered away the inheritance he was left to kick-start a career in the civil services.

By 1909, Hitler witnessed poverty up, close and personal. The winter of 1909 brought him an unexpected gift from an aunt, using which he began to paint Vienna's spectacular scenery using watercolors for a business associate. Hitler made enough survival money until he left for Munich in 1913. There was a general feeling of anti-Semitism among German working class nationalists, which didn't escape Hitler, though this remained under the surface until after World War I.

His early conundrum can be attributed to the fact that Hitler shared business and personal relationships with several Jews in Vienna. He was partly dependent on them for a living, which led to a rather complex equation about his real feelings for Jews. His strong anti-Semitic ideology came to the fore only during the World War I conflict, which shocked many who knew him closely.

Though he was fairly dependent on Jews for accommodation and money, Hitler couldn't escape the mainstream media's lopsided portrayal of Jews topped with stereotypes. They were made scapegoats in almost every issue plaguing the German population. The anti-Semitism had consumed several middle-class Germans in Vienna and Hitler began to attribute all the challenges in his life to the existence of Jews.

Hitler was fairly convinced that it was actually a Jewish professor who rejected his application when he sought to enroll at the Academy of Arts. He believed that his mother's death was due to the incapability of a Jewish doctor. When Adolf Hitler cleaned snow paths for large homes in the city, he assumed that only Jews had occupied these houses and hated them for it.

He left no stone unturned while mentioning his stint in Vienna as "five years of hardship and misery" in Mein Kampf. Hitler explicitly stated that all his challenges and tough times in Vienna were due to Jews, and in his own words, it was then that he began to hate them.

By 1910, Adolf Hitler was completely wrapped in the anti-Semitic ideology. Though historians argue that his hatred for Jews only developed after the First World War, there's no denying that the seeds were embedded pretty early during his time in Vienna.

Early Political Influences

Adolf Hitler was deeply impacted by two political leaders, including the German racist nationalism led by the Upper Austrian Pan-German political George von Schonerer, and Karl Lueger (Mayor of Vienna). Lueger was in power when Hitler came to Vienna, and espoused an anti-Semitism which was more real-world than ideological. It was during his stay in Vienna that he gradually began believing that Jews were the fundamental cause of all the ills plaguing the Germans, including chaos related to society, economy, politics, and culture.

Nevertheless, it embedded a staunch anti-Jewish rhetoric within the middle and lower class Germans who began to view them as enemies. While Schonerer was content with the nationalism of the elitist student fraternity, Lueger focused on mobilizing mass support from the working class crowd. He knew how to translate their emotions/beliefs into powerful political gains. Hitler's political strategy borrowed the nuances of both these leaders – his ideology was largely influenced by Schonerer, while his tactics were borrowed from Lueger.

In the summer of 1913, Hitler left for Munich with some inheritance money with the objective of escaping military service. He later went on to state that the only reason he did not desire service of the Habsburg Empire was owing to the fact that it was made up of mixed races. Later during the same year, Hitler had the police coming knocking on his door with a notice for evading military service from the Austrian government. Since he failed the medical examination, Hitler wasn't inducted into the military.

His medical report had stated Hitler to be too weak for tasks such as carrying weapons. For someone who was exceptionally good at gymnastics in school, this was attributed to years of living in food and sleep deprived conditions.

World War I

When the First World War began, Hitler crossed the Austrian border and traveled to Germany to fight for the German forces. He had a less elaborate medical examination that deemed him fit to be a part of the armed forces. World War I is said to be the turning point in Adolf Hitler's life since this is what gave a renewed purpose to his life. He was committed to the pursuit of serving Germany. Hitler acted as the dispatch runner on the Belgium-France Western Front.

It was a fairly risky job as there were constant enemy fire in these regions. His main duty was to pass on messages to officers on the front lines. Hitler wasn't one of the most popular soldiers among peers owing to his passion for trench warfare, unlike his colleagues who condemned war-like situations. After a period of four years, he shot up to the corporal rank, which wasn't considered too impressive. People attributed this to his underdeveloped social skills and inability to attract a decent following. Despite his unpopularity, Hitler did win favor with his seniors for his hard work and bravery.

Adolf Hitler wasn't the mighty Fuhrer who's thought itself made people shudder in his days as a soldier. Though he did win a few bravery awards and impressed his superiors, Hitler was known to be sloppy and highly unmilitary-like in his demeanor. Nevertheless, he was known to be ever willing for action when it came to the hazardous assignments, despite having had a few near death encounters.

He was not known to possess good interpersonal communication skills and was at best awkward in social situations, which seems a bit ironical considering Hitler went on to become one of the most influential and persuasive speakers of his time. He rose to fame quickly owing to his impassioned speeches, histrionics, and slick persuasion tactics.

Unlike his co-soldiers, Adolf Hitler seldom grumbled about the food or the sub-par living conditions. While soldiers discussed women, Hitler preferred discussions revolving around history, wars, and art. He never requested for leave, neither did he ever receive packages from back home. According to observers and fellow soldiers, Adolf Hitler appeared to try too hard to be in the good books of his seniors. In general, he was a loner who was known to get lucky.

On October 7, 1916, lady luck stopped smiling on Hitler and he was injured by a fragment in the leg during the Somme Battle. He was subsequently admitted to a hospital, which was his first stint away from war in two years. After recovery, Hitler was assigned lighter tasks in Munich. He was stunned by the anti-war rhetoric and apathy by German masses. Like all the woes gripping Germany, he squarely blamed the Jews for inspiring this feeling among Germans, which led them to undermine Germany's war efforts.

This notion of a Jewish anti-war conspiracy only added to Hitler's already impassioned anti-Semitic views formed in Vienna, which sowed the seed for an everlasting hatred for them. Raged and disappointed with the apathy showed by civilians, Hitler requested to be sent back to the war front.

Like all his country folks, Hitler was confident of Germany's victory in the First World War. When he was recuperating in the army hospital after being partially blinded by gas, Hitler heard the news of Germany's surrender. By his own admission, he wept for hours out of rage and humiliation.

Hitler's morale had now collapsed and he became severely depressed by Germany's dwindling hopes of emerging victorious in the war. He would be seated for hours engaged in deep thinking in his tent, and then suddenly run out screaming about certain invisible enemies of the Germans (mainly the Jews and Marxists).

The end of the First World War spelled the fact that Hitler now had to make his way into the civilian life where there were zero career prospects awaiting him. When he left the military hospital after completing his treatment, Hitler believed that the Jews alone were responsible for the humiliation faced by Germany in the war. He saw it as sheer betrayal and back-stabbing on their part, and his hatred only strengthened.

If you closely observe the instances in the formative life of Adolf Hitler, it isn't tough to connect the dots and see how he eventually became the way he did. All through his life, he was subjected to various political ideas and race/group identities, the most damning of which were the anti-Semitic seeds planted in his mind during his early life in Vienna. This led to him terming the entire Jewish race as inferior and rotten. His love for warfare resurfaced time and time again until it reached the pinnacle of utter doom fascination during the Second World War. His early life sufficiently establishes the backdrop that ultimately led to one of the worst catastrophes in human history – the Holocaust.

Chapter 2: How Hilter Became a Leader

During the summer of 1913, Adolf Hitler left for Munich and got accepted to the 16th Bavarian Infantry Regiment after he applied to serve as part of the German army. Though Hitler was still an Austrian citizen, he was inducted into the armed forces in August 1914. He spent much of his early service tenure away from the battlefront. There are some reports about how Hitler exaggerated his actual field time. Regardless, it's an undeniable fact that he was there for a large number of important battles, and would end up being severely hurt in the battle of Somme.

The Great Depression in Germany offered Hitler a strategic political opportunity in Germany. Germany was receptive to various government models including parliamentary republic and extremist systems.

1n 1932, Hitler decided to run for the German presidency. His opponent would be a Mister Paul von Hindenburg. Hitler emerged the runner-up in both rounds – the vote and final count. The results were Hitler's first foray into political leadership. Hindenburg went on to nominate Adolf Hitler as chancellor, although reluctantly, to foster political fairness. Hitler utilized his position to forge a strong de facto legally recognized dictatorship.

The Leader Emerges

After war broke out in August 1914, he served as a dispatch runner. Hitler proved to be an extremely courageous and able soldier, which won him the first Iron Cross bravery award and the Black Wound Badge. He was injured twice and temporality blinded due to the German Revolution of 1918, and the nation's military setback during World War I.

After recovery, Hitler was sufficiently convinced that he was fate's chosen one to rescue a once glorious state from the throes of disgrace. He strongly condemned the Versailles Treaty and sought to free Germany from its punitive tentacles.

It was in the summer of 1919 that Adolf Hitler witnessed the revolution of a small yet significant group called the German Worker's Party. He became a part of the political outfit on September 16, 1919, and subsequently called it the Nationalist Socialist German Worker's Party. He firmly established himself as the party's head by July 1921.

Hitler's mighty oratory skills were unveiled once he became the main spokesperson of the Nationalist Socialist German Workers' Party. He also contributed a brand new symbol to the party – the Swastika (a traditional Hindu symbol signifying prosperity). Other qualities that worked in his favor were his boisterousness, conviction, and histrionics laden speeches. This firmly established him as the German Fuhrer (German for leader) with more than 3,000 party members in comparison with the original strength of 40.

Under Adolf Hitler's leadership, the Nationalist Socialist German Worker's Party, or the Nazi Party, expanded into a significant mass movement and established a totalitarian rule over Germany from 1933 to 1945.

The party was segregated into strong squads such as the storm troopers called, the Sturmabteilung, and Hitler's own black-shirt bodyguards, known as the Schutzstaffel. His propaganda revolved around 'internal enemies' who were responsible for signing the Treaty of Versailles. According to Adolf Hitler, these people were to be blamed for Germany's internal woes.

The Racist Ideology

His disagreement of the Treaty of Versailles led to his political socialist ideology of the supremacy of the "pure" Aryan race. Hitler constantly reinforced the purity of the Germanic or Aryan race and prorogated that the race must retain its purity and not be diluted by other inferior races in order to be able to rule the entire world someday. The "perfect Aryan", according to Hitler was blue-eyed, above average height, and blonde.

Adolf Hitler fancied himself as a profound and intense thinker. He was convinced about his ability to understand the most complex problems in the world. Hitler firmly believed that an individual's characteristics such as skills, attitude, personality, and more are a direct result of his/her race. In his opinion, all races held particular traits that they invariably transferred to the subsequent generation through genetics. No person could rise above his racial make-up.

For Hitler and later his followers (the Nazis), a race could be preserved only through reproduction and acquiring land for supporting and feeding the growing population. They believed in the stringent enforcement of preserving the unique gene pool and racial characteristics of the "pure" Aryan race. According to them, the struggle for space and survival naturally led to constant military confrontations and violent clashes. Hence, war is – to them – an inevitable part of human survival. Hitler began to view the Jews as not belonging to a religion but an entire race. The Nazis assigned a huge number of unflattering stereotypes to Jews. It was in their opinion not a religious belief, but an entire race of biologically unchanging beings determined by an impure Jewish heritage. He fanned flames of the German masses by getting people to take immense pride in their superior racial lineage and fight for their supremacy over other inferior races trying to deteriorate their racial make-up.

Maintaining racial purity was central to Hitler's philosophy since according to the Nazi view, intermingling with other races leads to the bastardization or degradation of a race to a stage where it actually starts losing its most distinguishing characteristics. Hitler was of the view that losing his race's most distinct features and the inability to defend it by procuring land spelled extinction for the Germanic Aryan Race. Territory was important in the pursuit of safeguarding one's race, since space was needed to accommodate an ever-increasing population. Hitler feared his race would face stagnation and ultimately extinction if he didn't do anything about it.

Hitler Arrested

In 1923, the near collapse of the Weimar Republic government led Hitler to demand a Bavarian government overthrow in Munich. The notorious Beer Hall Putsch is where over 3,000 of Hitler's men swarmed into a huge beer hall and tried to overthrow the present Munich government. Hitler was arrested on February 26, 1924, and sentenced to be imprisoned for five years. However, he was released within nine months.

The Putsch failure and a Nazi Party ban made Hitler vow to come back with a vengeance, with the police and armed forces completely under his control. The Nazi Party ban was eventually lifted in 1925 and Adolf Hitler regained his right to conduct public speeches.

Owing to the Great Depression in 1928 and looming fears of a dwindling German economy, people decided against voting for Hitler's Nazi Party. This was a huge jolt to their fortunes and ambitions of power. Hitler ended up winning a disappointing 12 seats. However, despite the humongous defeat, the Nazis strategically began to woo the army, media, and industrial circles. Adolf Hitler ended up garnering a lot of publicity as a result.

He was known to be sharp, cunning, incisive, and manipulative. Hitler was well-known for his ability to stir up patriotic sentiments and the need for a powerful leadership through mass persuasion. Few leaders in world history have been able to use the art of persuasion to fulfill their goals as effectively and strategically as Hitler. In other words, he presented himself as the magic potion that would cure all their ills. He pitched himself as the ultimate savior of the Germans and the Germanic race.

Predictably, his party won the elections in 1930 with a sweeping majority (107 seats). He applied for German citizenship and was a presidential candidate in the 1931 elections, only to end up defeated against Von Hindenburg. However, not the ones to sit back and accept defeat, Hitler sought to build the party into a formidable force.

The Nazis rose as Germany's largest political party in 1932, with a whopping fourteen million votes in their kitty. Hitler hopped onboard as Germany's Chancellor on January 30, 1933. Once firmly entrenched in the throes of power, Hitler galloped. He did everything from eliminating rivals to abolishing trade unions to removing Jews from key social and political positions. He went on to establish a clear majority in the last documented 'democratic' German elections in 1933. This was achieved through intimidation, planned terror tactics, and smooth persuasion.

In August 1934, post the death of Von Hindenburg, Hitler was the uncontested leader of the Third Reich and assumed the complete power of the state. The next four years witnessed Adolf Hitler enjoying a host of local and global success, including outdoing political rivals overseas, and beating the opposition back home. He went on to nullify the Treaty of Versailles and sought to build his army by engaging in heavy recruitment. His army strength was now five-fold more than the actual permissible figure. Hitler leant his military support to the Spanish forces, owing to which they ended up winning in 1939.

Hitler introduced the German armament scheme that gave German citizens the opportunity to enjoy full employment in Germany. He carried out uninhibited military expansion and reiterated foreign policy victories such as the famous Rome-Berlin Pact (1936), the Austrian Anschluss, and the Sudeten Germans liberation. This brought Hitler to the pinnacle of power, where he felt he rightfully belonged.

Hitler's strategies forced the French and British to disregard the Munich Agreement of 1938, and the subsequent Czechoslovakian dismantlement of 1939. Hitler trained his guns on Poland next. Poland was an ally of France and Britain. Adolf Hitler went on to strategically sign a non-aggression treaty with Soviet Russia, which he subsequently violated.

Chapter 3: Hitler's Beliefs and Political Views

The dictionary definition of Nazism is "the ideology and policies of Adolf Hitler and his Nationalist Social German Worker's Party from 1921 to 1945." Hitler reiterated the superiority of the pure Germanic Aryan race, and believed in its responsibility as the "Master Race" to rule over the entire world. The race's roots could be traced back to the Aryan Indo-Europeans, who were Nordic in physical characteristics and German in ancestry. According to the Nazi theory, this race was naturally superior to all other races and hence deserved their rightful dominance over all social and political aspects.

Hitler's Political Influences

Hitler was impressed with DAP founder Anton Drexler's anti-capitalist, anti-Semitic, and anti-Marxist views. He was adept at using prevailing populist agendas such as using scapegoats for economic hardships faced by the German population. He shot to fame with his notorious impassioned speeches against the Treaty of Versailles, political rivals, and Jews/Marxists. He used personal magnetism for driving his ideology and political propaganda through impassioned public speeches.

Adolf Hitler firmly believed in the Fuhrerprinzip model of leadership. The principle entailed complete obedience of subordinates to the commands given by their superiors. There is no scope for dissent or rebellion. Hitler viewed his party and subsequently the government as a pyramid structure, which placed the leader at the apex.

The Nazi Party ranks weren't determined through democratic elections. Positions were quickly fulfilled by the higher rank members, who demanded undisputed and absolute obedience to the leader's command. There was no place for consensus or joint decision making. The party leader issued orders, which were to be diligently followed by all party members.

Mein Kampf

Several historians are of the view that Mein Kampf (Hitler's autobiography) summarizes his entire political philosophy and world ideologies, the crux of which is that Germany should rule the world as a superpower or it will perish. Inside Mein Kampf's pages, Adolf Hitler has elaborately described his struggle for helping Germany gain domination over the world. It also mentions his staunch views about the racial, social, political, and cultural conflict between the Jews and the Nordic Aryans, including a strong need for the racial purification of the Germanic Aryan population.

In Hitler's opinion, Germany required Lebensraum or extra living space which could efficiently nurture the German population's "historic destiny". This was fundamental to Adolf Hitler's foreign policies. Hitler wrote extensively about his hatred towards what he termed as the "world's twin evils" – Judaism and Marxism. He explained his goal of eradicating both the ills and unifying the
German population for achieving the same.

Hatred for Socialism

Hitler had a profound hatred for Germany's Social Democratic party, which in his opinion fostered deep class conflicts by sacrificing national interests and unity. In *Mein Kampf*, Adolf Hitler expresses hostility towards the Social Democratic movement. In his opinion, the working men were merely pawns of a purportedly created system for furthering the political gains of the party leaders. He believed the working men were being insidiously exploited and corrupted by an ideology that has no place in nationalism.

He also severely despised the Social Democratic movement for their excessive reliance on internalization and overseas trade. It was precisely one of the reasons why Hitler developed a deep hatred for Jews, since many of them led the Social Democracy Party.

Hitler's definition of socialism was grossly different from how it was traditionally defined. In his ideological framework, it wasn't a particular economic system but more of a means of self-preservation or conserving nationalism/national pride.

Nationalism and Ethnic Culture

Hitler refused to offer validity to trade unions or working classes. His disregard for working class movements, in general, is legendary. Once in power, Adolf Hitler completely went back on all that he had promised to do for the masses. They got rid of collective bargaining and declared the workers' rights to go on strike illegal. He overthrew trade unions with an outfit called the Labor Front, which was essentially a convenient arm of the Nazi Party. According to its manifesto, the body was created to ensure "every individual should be able to perform the maximum of work."

Hitler perceived German culture as all-encompassing and collective, not defined by individuals. For him, German culture or the "pure" Aryan Race were closely entwined with Germany's boundaries. For him, too, Germany was essentially a race, and the country's boundaries and race were not mutually exclusive.

For Adolf Hitler, the perfect Aryan is he who doesn't think twice before giving up his personal liberties in the larger interests of the community. Hitler's 25-Point program explicitly stated the importance of national interest (not exclusive from the German Aryan race and German culture) over personal gains/freedom. He staunchly believed that the nation could be permanently healthy only when Germans placed common interest before self-serving interests.

Hitler's idea of nationalism was based on common blood and physical characteristics, and folk community. What he termed as nationalism can be viewed as disguised racism. Consider these lines from Mein Kampf; "The German Reich as a state must embrace all Germans and has the task, not only of assembling and preserving the most valuable stocks of basic racial elements in this people, but slowly and surely raising them to a dominant position."

For Hitler, the Aryan race was the most evolved and perfect race in the world. He went as far as attributing developments in technology, science, culture, and arts solely to the genius of Aryans. His speeches and writings were peppered with how the barbarians or non-Aryans would take over the world and the Aryan race would become extinct if people didn't do anything about it.

In Adolf Hitler's opinion, to expedite world progress, it was important to keep the Aryan race pure by disallowing interbreeding within races, particularly between those of Aryan and Jewish descent. Hitler was also critical of the Pan-German revolution in Austria since, in his opinion, imposing German language on people doesn't make them German. He believed the Germans were citizens by race or birth and not merely a cultural legacy or language.

Hitler's views were reflective of the law of the jungle that life, where survival of the fittest is the only norm. He viewed different human races as species that would have to intensely compete with each other for space, territory, food, and power. Yale historian Timothy Synder, the author of *Black Earth: The Holocaust as History and Warning* stated that for Hitler, "the only morality was fidelity to race."

Parliament, Internalization and Capitalism

For Hitler, internalization and democracy were closely entwined. Prior to Hitler's rule, German democracy was all about dependence on the outer world. He staunchly opposed this. For Adolf Hitler, economic independence was the organic outcome of a healthy national state. In the 1930's this seemed a highly implausible idea. No nation or region was fully economically self-sufficient, since food was almost always imported from neighboring nations. A completely self-reliant nation was Hitler's objective, where national production and self-consumption were a norm for creating the perfect balance.

Hitler despised all forms of parliamentary and democratic rule. He has unambiguously criticized corrupt representatives and parliamentarians since he believed nominations were based not on a person's abilities or character, but merely on the whims and fancies of the party. In his own opinion, he sought to liberate Germany from the tentacles of parliamentary democracy not to stifle free spirit, but to create a stronger nation that was capable of ruling over the world.

Hitler strongly believed that what ailed Germany's parliamentary system was that it didn't comprise of a group of intelligent and knowledgeable people, neither did it make efforts to do so. Adolf Hitler's view was that mere parliamentarians were a group of non-capable entities who were completely reliant on others for their views and could be easily misled. Hitler believed that the perfect government is one that doesn't make it tough for people of caliber to attain success and reach influential positions.

Capitalism was scorned at by Hitler. He was critical of capitalism since he believed capitalists wielded complete control over the masses. In a 1940 Berlin speech, Adolf Hitler clearly stated how capitalists cared about the masses only when they needed their votes during elections. War rationing was at its peak in Germany during the 1940s.It was during this time that capitalists and traders began hoarding goods and sought restrictions on the fair distribution of goods.

Hitler demanded that the profits of large industries be shared to ensure equal distribution of income. However, the party never formally implemented the demand. Hitler was also deeply critical of countries such as the United States, which he thought were the epitome of selfishness, where a small section of people ruled under the garb of democracy.

What's interesting to any observer is the fact that Adolf Hitler called his party 'National Socialist Party' even though he was strongly opposed to socialism, which has its roots firmly entrenched in Marxism. Also, Nationalist Socialist in itself comes across as an oxymoron, with nationalist defining the right wing and socialist indicating the left-wing. Socialism itself is an innately internationalist ideology; borders are commonly seen as irrelevant as opposed to class, where the central struggle is seen by socialism as one between capitalists and their workers. Borders are seen by socialists as a mere distraction to the true liberatory issue in society: that of a society without capital being directed and controlled by a select few. The view of the National Socialists was diametrically opposed to this: they saw race as society's central struggle, not class, and their entire ideology was created in order to preserve and spread the German borders.

Chapter 4: World War II

On September 1, 1939, the German forces launched an attack on Poland and drove away the Polish from their territory after their leadership tried to obtain Germany's 'free living space' or Lebensraum as it was referred to. Phase I of World War II was characterized by the Blitzkrieg technique, which comprised sudden airfield attacks or strikes on military installations. This involved the usage of mobile armor and advanced bomber battle aircraft. Hitler's superior military prowess resulted in Poland being brought under siege in less than 30 days, and France, Belgium, and Holland being subjugated in the subsequent six weeks.

Joining Forces with the Italians

The downfall of France dwindled Britain's confidence, but it refused to toe the line, much to Hitler's chagrin. Adolf Hitler's first setback during World War II was the Battle of Britain, in which the RAF foiled Luftwaffe's attempts of gaining supremacy over Britain's skies. Hitler was forced to retreat and delay the British invasion. In the meanwhile, he joined forces with Italian allies who were in conflict in Northern Africa. Hitler captured some portions of Yugoslavia, Crete and Greece.

Although there was a non-aggression Treaty in place with Soviet Russia, Hitler conquered the Russian territories in June 1941 with the intention of weakening the British forces.

America Enters World War II

With America entering World War II in 1941, Britain snubbed Germany's attempt to gain dominance over the European continent. This led Hitler to implement the 'Final Solution of the Jewish Question', which was being deliberated for a couple of years. It called for the complete eradication of the Jewish population. The strategy was expedited when Britain refused to accept subordination even in the face of explicit threats from Hitler about the extermination of Jews around the world.

It started with Jew-eradication measures that were carried out in different areas of Germany and Poland, where the Jew population was sent to various concentration camps to be eliminated in huge numbers. Hitler did not spare Bolshevism either. He targeted Russian armed forces with the aim of eliminating the Bolshevist roots.

The Infamous Holocaust

The term holocaust originates from the Greek words – holos (translated whole) and kaustos (meaning burned). Traditionally, it was used to signify the burning of a sacrificial offering on an ancient altar. The term assumed an altogether different and horrifying meaning after the mass murder of about 6-million European Jews, in addition to members of other persecuted groups by Hitler's Nazi regiment during World War II. Hitler's strong anti-Semitic views were well-known by then. His emphasis on racial purity and preventing the denigration of the superior Aryan race finally led to what the Nazis called the "final solution" during the Second World War. Under the garb of war, the Nazi's long awaited Holocaust plan came to be implemented. Concentration camps were specially created in various captured German-occupied Polish territories.

Hitler's men created more than 100 camps within the country and over 100 outside it to subject thousands of Jews to the most horrifying and gruesome methods of torture, including systematically eliminating them using starvation, shooting, and poisonous gas. There were instances of Jews being herded in trucks and mass murdered by specially trained firing squads. Several large camps such as Auschwitz gained notoriety for witnessing over 1,000,000 deaths.

Hitler cleverly steered clear from giving any written orders for exterminating the Jewish civilian population. He also evaded openly talking about murdering Jews within his loyal entourage. However, there has been clinching evidence of his deep involvement in a staunchly anti-Jewish rhetoric, which gradually elevated to murderous rage. Adolf Hitler's objective of radicalizing persecution of the Jews was evident during his impassioned, hate speeches in the earlier stages of his political career.

Hitler was completely involved in ordering the mass execution of Jews in Poland between 1939 and 1940, according to various historians. He was constantly preoccupied with drafting multiple and careful deportation plans for giving fruition to his 'final solution.' He was kept in the loop about mass murders of Jew civilians in various territories. Hitler openly referred to the obliteration of European Jews. It is preposterous to assume that the heavy-duty preparations for systematically eliminating Jews in various, especially set-up extermination camps in occupied territories were implemented without his knowledge or sanction.

A written order signed July 31, 1941, from Hermann Goering (Hitler's commander) to Reinhard Heydrich (chief of SD) mentioned a pointed reference to the need to offer a final solution for the troubling Jewish question. Since September 1914, every Jew on German or occupied territory was assigned a yellow star, thus making them obvious targets. They were systematically and strategically deported to Poland in huge numbers.

There were several on-going experiments with different mass killing techniques within the Polish camps. In August 1914, Nazi officials subjected 500 prisoners of war to death using the deadly pesticide Zyklon-B. SS (Schutzstaffel – a paramilitary outfit of Hiter's Nazi Party) placed a big order for the lethal gas with a leading national pest-control firm, thus pointing to an oncoming Holocaust.

The Nazis tried their level best to keep the camps a secret, considering the nature of the operation. However, with the staggering number of victims, it became near impossible to hide it. Eyewitnesses came forward with elaborate accounts of Nazi brutalities across various camps in Poland. The lack of action despite being privy to information of these atrocities was attributed to the fact that the Allied governments were more focused on emerging victorious in the war. Another reason cited by historians was a general sentiment of incomprehension and disbelief that atrocities on such a huge scale could ever occur. More than 2-million Jew civilians were killed in Auschwitz alone, and approximately 12,000 Jews were massacred daily.

Personal diaries of Nazi strategist and propagandist Joseph Goebbels and the Gestapo Chief Heinrich Himmler discovered from the Soviet archives reveal that Hitler ordered the genocide of Jews on December 12, 1941, during a Nazi governors' meeting. Goebbels explicitly stated in his diary writings: "With regards to the Jewish question, the Fuhrer decided to make a clean sweep."

While the Italians failed in the Middle East conflict, the United States entered the Second World War, thus spelling the beginning of Germany's downfall. Though the signs were obvious, Hitler refused to view it in its correct perspective. He believed his military was becoming indecisive and inadequate. Adolf Hitler launched into hysterical bouts of anger and irrational brooding spells. As a result, his health began to deteriorate.

Chapter 5: Notable Moments in Hitler's Life

1922: The German National Movement

A call for Hitler's National Movement in 1922 was one of the most significant landmarks in Adolf Hitler's political career. The movement struck a chord with middle-class Germans since they staunchly believed that their internal state structure was more Semitic than Germanic. All the top positions in the economic and other crucial sectors were held by the Jews.

Hitler's national movement emphasized how their own people were being gradually destroyed by the class struggle, political party disputes, and Bolshevism. Hitler stated clearly in a speech on the 18th of September 1922 delivered in Munich, that the only germ of this growing disease gripping Germany were the Jews. He also went on to elaborate how the Jews contributed towards the disintegration of Germany.

During the now infamous Munich speech, Adolf Hitler emphasized how Jewish bankers were adversely affecting the sacred German nationalist cause with their vested interests. Hitler demanded in no uncertain terms that every Jew who made their way into Germany after the First World War should be expelled.

1920: Nazi Party Formed

Hitler made fervent attempts to make the German Worker's party (which he joined in 1919) succeed. The party comprised of an executive committee that had seven officials, including Hitler. In an effort to grow the party's strength, Adolf Hitler started creating invitations and distributing them among existing committee members, asking them to give it to friends. However, very few people ended up attending the public meetings.

Hitler then struck upon a plan. They inserted an advertisement in a popular anti-Semitic newspaper published in Munich. While other committee members were apprehensive about filling up the beer cellar where the meeting had been organized, more than hundred people crowded into it.

Though other committee members were unsure of Hitler's oratory skills, he won over everyone in the audience with his emotionally laced and almost hysterical speech style. This was one of the most defining moments in his political career.

Hitler won the election with a clean sweep and went on to become the head of a brand new political party, referred to as the Nazi Party, though it was officially called the National Socialist German Workers Party. The party staunchly believed that equality was the birthright only of the Germans and not migrants or Jews.

Adolf Hitler strategically understood how a strong political party that opposed a Communist agenda could have a huge impact on gaining the support of German nationals. Hitler changed the name of the German Workers' Party to Nationalist Socialist German Workers' Party, nicknamed Nazi. By the beginning of 1921, the party had more than three thousand members.

1923: The Bavaria Beer Hall Movement

When Germany's economy started witnessing its downfall in the 1920's, Hitler seized the opportunity to lead his men to the famous Bavaria beer hall where local government officials had planned to hold a meeting on November 8th, 1923.

The Nazis simply went on to capture the converging politicians and marched to the Bavarian Armed Forced Ministry building. Though there was open firing by the police and Hitler lost his associate during the riot, the incident was his first brush with national fame. Germans all over the country finally began to sit up and take notice of an emerging leader.

1925: Mein Kampf Gets Published

Although Mein Kampf is widely known to be Hitler's autobiography, he never really sat down to write the book in a traditional sense. Instead, the accounts mentioned in the book were dictated to his associate Rudolph Hess during Hitler's time in prison (1923-24) and then at a Berchtesgaden inn. Therefore, reading his autobiography is more akin to hearing Hitler speak about his life, political ideologies, and dreams for Germany.

The initial title chosen by Hitler for his autobiography was "Four and a Half Years of Struggle against Lies, Stupidity, and Cowardice". Since his publisher was a Nazi himself, he shortened the title to "Mein Kampf" or *My Battle*. In the book, Hitler has unambiguously divided people into multiple categories on the basis on their physical characteristics. He has also gone a step further and established a superior and inferior order for humans based on their physical attributes.

On the top of the pyramid, according to Hitler, is the German man or the Germanic Aryan with his milk-white skin, blue eyes, and blond hair. He has often referred to the Aryan race as the supreme or master human race.

When Mein Kampf was first published in 1925, it barely sold any copies. People had been awaiting a book filled with juicy details or tell-all background stories. However, what they received was verbose, hard to follow reading matter, and almost erratic paragraphs.

This changed completely after Hitler became the German Chancellor. Millions of copies of Mein Kampf sold within a short span of time. One of the factors responsible for the sudden burst of sales was that it was considered appropriate to gift the book to newlyweds, graduates, and on other celebratory occasions, though barely any Germans read the entire book. Although he became rich from the royalty proceeds of his autobiography, Hitler considered it a bad move since the book comprised of several crucial revelations, which he believed were better off without being mass publicized.

1929-30: Nazis Come to Power Following the Great Depression

After the Wall Street stock market collapsed On October 29, 1929, it sent the world's financial markets into a shockwave, with widespread disastrous effects. The German economy was especially hit since it was heavily dependent on foreign trade and capital, and mainly loans from The United States of America.

Overnight, Germany's heavy loans were due and exports quickly dried up. The well mechanized German industrial system came to a halt. German middle-class workers were quickly sacked and savings accounts dissolved. Inflation hit the German market hard and families found it tough to make ends meet.

Middle-class Germany was in shambles and was desperately looking for a knight in shining armor. Thus, The Great Depression set a wonderful political stage for Hitler to prove himself as the messiah of the German masses. Adolf Hitler's moment of glory had arrived.

September 14th, 1930 was set as the election day, and Hitler knew he had to make the most of his campaigning. Germans by now were tired of being at the receiving end of economic weakness and persistent suffering. They were desperate for change, and they were willing to accept anyone who made claims to change their fortune – even someone like Adolf Hitler.

1929: Hitler and Eva Braun Meet

Eva Braun was born to Friedrich Braun and Franziska Kronberger, who both belonged to respectable, upper-class Bavarian Catholic clans in Munich. At 17, Eva took up a job as an office assistant and model for the official photographer of the Nazi Party, Heinrich Hoffman. Eva and Hitler met at the photographer's studio in Munich in 1929. Braun described Hitler to her associates as a "gentleman of a certain age with a funny mustache, a light-colored English overcoat, and carrying a big felt hat." Hitler greatly appreciated Eva's eye color, which he felt was exactly the same as his mother's. It is a known fact that

Eva Braun's family was vehemently opposed to her relationship with Adolf Hitler, at least during the initial stages.

For security reasons, Hitler was introduced to Braun under the nickname Herr Wolf. A few days into the meeting, Eva consented to following the leader to his luxurious Alps mountain retreat. Since her parents strongly objected to the match, Eva chose to be Hitler's mistress. For the next decade and a half, she continued to live in the lap of opulence, while Hitler unleashed his terror.

1932: Hitler Granted German Citizenship, Runs for Presidency

In 1932, Hitler decided to contest against Paul von Hindenburg for the presidency. The "Freedom and Bread" campaign turned out to be a huge success. Joseph Goebbels, Hitler's associate launched a massive propaganda campaign for Adolf Hitler, outdoing even their previous 1930 efforts. There was no escaping the Nazi posters, the whirlwind of impassioned speeches, and the hundreds of rallies across the nation. The Nazis went all out to distribute pamphlets and Nazi publications. Goebbels went a step further and started using slick technology for recording and distributing Hitler's photographs and films.

The people of Germany viewed the Nazis as the saviors of their heritage, pride, and future. After experiencing success in the momentous 1930 election, the Nazi party attracted thousands of new party members who were eager to be a part of Germany's new wave.

In 1932, a staggering six million Germans were unemployed. There was sheer confusion and rage in Berlin about the government's inability to meet the interests of German nationals. The fear of Marxism loomed large, thus gripping the working class with an uncertainty-laden future. Hindenburg failed to garner an absolute majority in the election thus paving the way for a run-off election.

1934: Adolf Hitler Declares Himself Fuhrer

After the death of President Hindenburg on August 2, 1934, Adolf Hitler completely overthrew the offices of the president and chancellor with a dictatorial seat by declaring himself The Fuhrer or Leader of a new Germany – The German or Third Reich. With almost no resistance from an already crumbling leadership, Germany's military oath was conveniently altered to become a statement that demanded complete obedience to Hitler's commands.

1938: Munich Agreement

The Munich Agreement was an understanding about Sudetenland, the area located along the Czech borders. This region was predominantly occupied by Czech-German citizens. The landmark agreement was undertaken in the presence of several European superpowers in Munich in the absence of Czech representatives. It was more an act of appeasement than an officious treaty.

The Munich Agreement was signed on September 30, 1938, though it was dated September 29th. The main objective of the conference was the discussion of Czechoslovakia's future under the circumstances of Hitler's dictatorial territory demands. The agreement was signed by Britain, France, and Germany, while Italy gave its consent for Sudetenland by Germans. Sudetenland was strategically important to Czechoslovakia as a majority of the region's defense borders were housed there.

1939 – 1945: German Occupation of Poland

The German-Polish Non-Aggression Pact was an international agreement between the Nazi Germans and the Second Polish Republic that was signed on January 26th, 1934. It pledged that both nations would come together to sort their issues through bilateral talks and renunciation of armed conflict for at least a decade. The previously strained relationship between Germany and Poland neutralized. Germany respected Poland's borders and made efforts towards ending a customs war that would be economically disastrous for both countries.

At the onset of the Second World War, Polish territory was segregated into Nazi Germany and the USSR. During the summer of 1941, the Nazis managed to successfully annex territories held by the Soviets after a series of attacks. However, after years of war, the Red Army gathered its bearings and began driving out the seemingly invincible Nazis not just from USSR but also other parts of Eastern Europe.

The Germans and Soviets were both indifferent to Polish people and culture, solely aiming to destroy them. More than 6 million Polish citizens (a staggering 22% of Poland's population, mostly civilians) lost their lives during Germany and USSR's deliberate, non-military tactics.

1940: France Surrenders to German Forces

The summer of 1940 witnessed Germany invading Norway and Denmark. Hitler's men then went on to attack France, annexing Luxembourg, Belgium, and Netherlands in the bargain. France eventually surrendered to the German forces on June 22, 1940. This victory propelled the Italian dictator, Mussolini, to join Hitler's side in the Second World War.

Britain continued to steadfastly evacuate France through seaways from the Dunkirk region. Adolf Hitler's peace proposals were shot down by the British, which was now led by the able Winston Churchill. Irked by this development, Hitler demanded a series of bombing raids in the United Kingdom. The great Battle of Britain was supposed to a prelude for Germany's bigger invasion plans in Britain.

The attacks started by attempting to destroy Britain's Royal Air Force and strategic radar bases that safeguarded South-East England. The Luftwaffe, however, wasn't successful in destroying the Royal Air Force. In October 1940, Hitler gave orders for bombing the British cities – London, Coventry, and Plymouth.

1941: Hitler Declares War on the United States

Hitler declared war against the mighty United States of America
on December 11, 1941, just four days following the Japanese
attack on Hawaii's Pearl Harbor. This rather ambitious move set
him against some of the mightiest nations in the world – the
planet's largest empire (British), the planet's most technically
advanced and financially secure superpower (United States),
and the planet's largest army (Soviet).

Historians believe that Hitler was keen on declaring war against
the United States for no other reason than the grandiosity of the
prospect. According to several reports, Hitler was thoroughly
excited by the idea of being at the helm of one of the greatest
wars in history.

In 1942, Hitler's grand plans of seizing the crucial Suez Canal
were sealed after they were defeated in the second El Alamein
battle. 1943 only made it worse for the German forces, with their
6th Army completely destroyed in the Stalingrad Battle. The
Battle of Kursk followed closely on the heels on the Stalingrad.
Hitler had lost his military judgment by now and wielded
decisions more erratically, which led to the economic and
military denigration of Germany. Hitler's health started
witnessing a downward spiral. His biographer Ian Kershaw and
several others believe that though it was never made public,
Hitler was down with Parkinson's.

1942: Mass Gassing Operations

A Nazi extermination camp (called Sobibór) was strategically set
up in Poland's Lublin area as part of the Reinhard operation.
Jews and Jewish Soviet prisoners of war were taken to the
Sobibór by train, following which they were stuffed inside the
gas chamber and suffocated with petrol engine exhaust.
According to Professor Scheffler, who was brought in as an
expert in the Hagen legal proceedings against the Nazis, the
death toll was at least 250,000. The site houses a museum and
memorial today.

1945: Hitler Commits Suicide

Hitler committed suicide on 30th April 1945 (more in the next chapter) by shooting himself with a pistol. His body was subsequently taken into the Reich Chancellery Garden by associates, who covered it with petrol and set it on fire alongside the body of Eva Braun (who joined Hitler in his death by consuming cyanide).

This signified the ultimate ruin of a civilization and the senseless destruction of human life for the purpose of power and a false racial arrogance. Adolf Hitler's tyrannical power play and misplaced ideologies destroyed the 'Greater Germanic Reich'.

Chapter 6: Hitler's Death

In early 1945, Germany's military situation deteriorated. Its downfall began when the Germans were defeated by the Allies in the landmark Ardennes Offensive. The Canadian and British military crossed the Rhine and entered the German commercial hub – Ruhr. The American military had already annexed Lorraine and was fast moving towards Mannheim and Mainz. In Italy, too, the German forces were gradually retreating northward as they were being intimidated by both American and British Commonwealth forces.

Adolf Hitler became bitter after Germany's First World War efforts collapsed. The things he witnessed during the war only went on to reinforce his passionate patriotism. Hitler believed that Germany had time and again been betrayed by its own civilians. It started in 1918 when Germany surrendered, in Hitler's opinion, due to Marxists and misguided civilians. He saw the Treaty of Versailles as highly humiliating, especially the Rhineland demilitarization and the clause where Germany was required to accept complete responsibility for beginning the conflict.

Hitler ruled over the fast collapsing Third Reich, and it was clear that the Berlin battle would be the final conflict for establishing supremacy in Europe. He went back to his Fuhrerbunker in Berlin in January 1945. On 18th April, 325,000 German soldiers were captured by the American forces, thus leaving the entryway to Berlin open.

The last defensive border safeguarding Berlin, Seelow Heights was about to be accessed by the Soviet armed forces after crossing the Oder. The Germans were left with no option but to get into full retreat mode, thus leaving no front lines open. Berlin was captured by the soviet forces on a rather momentous day – 20th April, which was Hitler's birthday. By 21st April the Red Army tankers accessed the outskirts of Berlin.

The German army was ill equipped to halt Marshall Zhukov's soldiers. They were completely outnumbered and the Red Army resorted to the use of mechanized armor, which was another jolt for the already struggling German forces. The German Army was no match for Marshall Zhukov's heavily equipped troops. Berlin's military and civilian war casualties reached an alarmingly high number.

Despite defeat staring him in the face, Adolf Hitler was adamant that the German forces would defeat Zhukov's army in Berlin. He spoke in grandiose terms about how the armored formations would completely destroy Zhukov right here in Berlin. The reality was grimmer than Hitler wanted to believe. Being in denial about an impending defeat, he refused to acknowledge the fact that his troops were now a bunch of tried and exhausted men who could do little to enliven Germany's sagging chances.

The smallest signs of peace or surrender were dealt with severely by Hitler's men. They shot everybody who put up a while flag signifying peace outside their home. Adolf Hitler firmly placed himself in a bunker just below the Reich Chancellery structure. The premises had been created with an advanced communication system. Staff officers continuously checked the proliferation of the Red Army by calling civilians randomly to check if their phone lines were functional.

On the morning of 28th April, Adolf Hitler received a document that Himmler, the leader of SS, had communicated to the Allies (Count Bernadette of the Swedish arm of the Red Cross) about a potential surrender. In the eyes of Hitler, Himmler had been one of his most loyal men. He went into a mad rage when Reuter confirmed the report. Hitler blamed another SS official Herman Fegelein who was in the bunker with him for being privy to the surrender information and not keeping Hitler in the loop about it. Fegelein initially denied knowing anything about the surrender but eventually admitted it in the face of intense pressure. He was not just stripped off all his ranks and medals, but was also shot at the Reich Chancellery Garden.

On the midnight of April 28th, Hitler wed Eva Braun. The wedding service was held in one of the private sitting rooms by a low-rank Nazi official who was authorized to perform civil weddings, and who asked Hitler and Braun if they belonged to the pure Aryan race. The register was signed by Goebbels and Bormann.

Eva Braun had spent a major part of her life waiting to marry Adolf Hitler, and she had no second thoughts on sharing death with him when he expressed his wish to her. She wanted to be with him in life and death. Hitler also wanted her to be with him in death since she was a significant part of his life for several years. Hitler is believed to have said just minutes before his death that, "Miss Braun, besides my dog Blondi, is the only one I can absolutely count on…"

On the night of 29th April, Hitler received the damning news that Berlin would cease to receive any more soldiers, and the city would be defeated at the hands of the Russians. General Welding who was in charge of protecting Berlin was of the view that his troops would give up combat due to their dwindling ammunition resources.

Though by now Hitler had already made up his mind about suicide being his and Eva's only resort, this bit of information only quickened the decision. Hitler received another piece of information that Mussolini's and his mistress Clara's body had been hung upside down in a Milan square after they were caught and shot in Italy. Adolf Hitler wanted to avoid this humiliation. He gave orders for his body to be burned after his death.

Hitler called for a meeting with his inner coverer in his ante-room chamber. Hearty farewells were exchanged here. He oversaw the poisoning of his pet dog Blondi and her pups. He retreated into his private room with Eva Braun after bidding farewell to the entire staff. On 30th April, at 15.15 Hitler shot himself (using a 7.65mm Walther pistol) with a gunshot that no one heard. Before shooting himself Hitler and Eva also consumed cyanide.

Hitler's valet Heinz Linge described in detail how he witnessed Hitler in an upright position on a messy blood soaked couch with blood trickling from his right temple. The pistol was lying on the floor. While Hitler had chosen to shoot himself along with consuming cyanide, Eva Braun preferred to leave her gun unused.

Hitler's men wrapped Hitler's body in a blanket and took it to the chancellery garden. Eva's body was kept beside Hitler's near the bunker exit. The bodies were soaked in petrol and set on fire in the presence of Goebbels, Bormann, and other Hitler aides. While Goebbels committed suicide, Borman is believed to have escaped to South America.

On May 2, 1945, Berlin finally surrendered. There are several contradictory reports about what become of Hitler's remains. While some historical researchers concluded (based on the Soviet archive information) that the bodies of Adolf Hitler, Eva Braun, and his associates were discreetly buried in a Rathenow, Brandenburg located grave, others believe that their remains were cremated and dispersed in a river by Soviet forces. The Russian Federal Security Service lists a human skull housed in its archives (publically exhibited in 2000) as Hitler's body remains. However, its veracity is being debated by historians.

Conclusion

Once again, thank you for choosing this book. I hope you found it to be a captivating and informative recount of the terrifying life of Adolf Hitler.

If you enjoyed the book, please take the time to leave a review on Amazon – it helps me to continue producing high quality books!

Thanks for reading, and don't forget to take a look at the other biographical books I have available on Amazon!